HISTORY'S
VILLAINS

IVAN
THE TERRIBLE

Don Nardo

BLACKBIRCH PRESS

An imprint of Thomson Gale, a part of The Thomson Corporation

THOMSON

GALE

Detroit • New York • San Francisco • San Diego • New Haven, Conn. • Waterville, Maine • London • Munich

THOMSON

™

GALE

© 2006 Thomson Gale, a part of The Thomson Corporation.

Thomson and Star Logo are trademarks and Gale and Blackbirch Press are registered trademarks used herein under license.

For more information, contact
Blackbirch Press
27500 Drake Rd.
Farmington Hills, MI 48331-3535
Or you can visit our Internet site at http://www.gale.com

LIBRARY OF CONGRESS CATALOGING-IN-PUBLICATION DATA

Nardo, Don, 1947–
  Ivan the terrible / by Don Nardo.
    p. cm. — (History's villains)
  Includes bibliographical references.
  ISBN 1-56711-900-X (hard cover : alk. paper)
1. Ivan IV, Czar of Russia, 1530–1584—Juvenile literature.. 2. Russia—Kings and rulers—Biography—Juvenile literature. 3. Russia—History—Ivan IV, 1533–1584—Juvenile literature. I. Title. II. Series.

DK106.N37 2005
947'.043'092—dc22

2005014118

Printed in the United States of America

Contents

INTRODUCTION:
THE BLOODBATH BEGINS

Sometime in the fall of 1566, a group of Russian nobles, or boyars, met in secret in the city of Moscow. These men decided to take their lives in their hands, not only for their own good but for the sake of their country. Carefully, they drew up a petition. It was addressed to the grand prince of Russia. The petition called on that ruler—Ivan IV—to stop the attacks he had recently launched against the boyar class.

The trouble had begun the year before. Indeed, 1565 had proved a turning point for the boyars, as well as for the Russian people in general. Before that date, Ivan had shown himself to be a strong leader who at times treated his enemies harshly. But most Russians had seen him as an effective and largely fair ruler. This view began to change when, early in 1565, he created a regiment of followers he called the *oprichniki*, or "separated ones." Blindly loyal to Ivan, they terrified all who encountered them. They wore black robes and rode large black horses. In addition to razor-sharp swords, they carried brooms, which symbolized their mission to sweep away all threats to their master.

The *oprichniki* also tied severed dogs' heads to their saddles. This gesture was intended to show that these men were ready to commit acts of extreme brutality for Ivan. And no sooner had he organized his band of henchmen when he began ordering such acts. The *oprichniki* rounded up any boyars and their followers whom the grand prince suspected of disloyalty. All were questioned under torture. Ivan himself often took part in these gruesome sessions. A European visitor to the Russian court witnessed some of them and later wrote:

> [Ivan] habitually [often] watches with his own eyes those who are being tortured and put to death. Thus it happens frequently that blood spurts onto his face. He is not in the least disturbed by the blood, but on the contrary, he is exhilarated by it and shouts "*Goida! Goida!*" ("Hurrah!"), and then all those around him shout: "*Goida! Goida!*"[1]

With a pair of wings clipped to his uniform, a top member of the oprichniki *prepares his men for an attack.*

5

A Fatal Error

Hoping to put an end to these horrors, the nobles who drafted the petition gathered their courage and sought an audience with the grand prince. A German observer named Albert Schlichting was serving as an interpreter for Ivan at the time. Schlichting witnessed the presentation of the petition and later jotted down its contents. "Most illustrious Tsar [emperor] and Lord," the petitioners began,

> why have you given orders to kill our innocent brethren? We have all served you loyally and spilled our blood for you! This is the way you reward us for our services? You throw the *oprichniki* at our throats, they pluck our brethren . . . from our midst, they commit outrages against us, they beat, stab, and strangle us, and in the end they will kill us all.[2]

Perhaps the petitioners believed they enjoyed strength in numbers. Nearly 300 of them signed and presented the petition. Surely, they likely reasoned, Ivan would be moved by the large number and lofty social status of the protesters. And this would force him to address the protesters' grievances in a reasonable way.

The petitioners had made a serious and ultimately fatal error, however. Ivan was moved, but his reaction was one of rage rather than reason. He immediately ordered his black-clad guards to arrest the protesters and take them to his dungeons. The three leading protesters were tortured and beheaded. Several others had their tongues cut out. Still others had one or more limbs amputated. In all, more than 200 of the petitioners were killed, and the rest were mutilated in some way.

A Reign of Terror

These poor souls were not alone. In the months and years that followed, Ivan's reign of terror not only continued but increased in size and ferocity. He accused former associates who had served him loyally for some time of plotting against him. They were killed horribly, often cut to pieces by the *oprichniki*. Equally innocent relatives, servants, and friends of the victims were tortured, raped, and killed. Soon, Ivan grew dissatisfied with the scale of his murders. He began thinking about wiping out entire cities. The enormous bloodbath that would inspire later generations to give him the nickname "the Terrible" had begun.

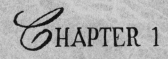

CHAPTER 1

IVAN'S CHILDHOOD AND RISE TO POWER

The man whom posterity would come to call Ivan the Terrible was born in the Terem Palace in Moscow on August 25, 1530. The child's official name was Ivan IV Vasilevich. He was named after his grandfather Ivan III, who had ruled the Russian kingdom from 1462 to 1505. Ivan III's son, Vasily III, had succeeded him on the throne and was still grand prince when his own son, Ivan IV, came into the world.

Ivan's mother, Elena Glinskaya, was Vasily's second wife. A number of the boyars who attended the Moscow court distrusted her because she was a foreigner. She came from Lithuania, then a prominent

Ivan IV was named for his grandfather Ivan III shown here in an eighteenth century drawing.

kingdom bordering Russia in the west, and they worried that her allegiance would always lie with the land of her birth. However, other boyars welcomed Elena. They were charmed by her beauty, intelligence, and pleasant demeanor and saw that she made their ruler, Vasily, happy.

All Russians certainly seemed happy when they learned of the birth of Elena's son Ivan. Church bells echoed through the streets and elaborate religious services and celebrations were held in Moscow and other nearby towns. Also, following custom, people lavished all sorts of gifts on the new baby.

Later chroniclers claimed that Ivan's birth was marked by omens as well. It was said that huge storms raged and the ground shook all across the Russian steppes. One later writer claimed that when a Russian messenger brought news of the child's birth to the neighboring kingdom of Kazan, the wife of the local ruler uttered a dire prophecy. The child had been born with two teeth, she said. "With one, he will devour us," she declared. "And with the other he will devour you,"[3] she told the Russian. These tall tales, however, appeared well after the grown-up Ivan had ravaged both Kazan and Russia. So their creators had the benefit of hindsight.

IVAN THE TERRIBLE

An Emerging Russian Nation

The reality is that at the time Ivan was born, no one in Russia or neighboring states had any idea what lay in store for him—or them. The leaders of these states

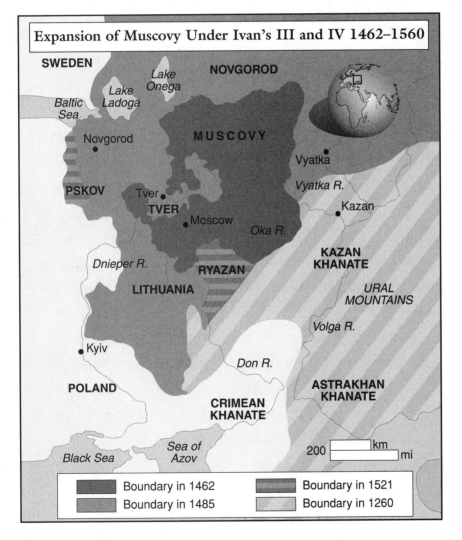

Expansion of Muscovy Under Ivan's III and IV 1462–1560

SWEDEN

NOVGOROD

Lake Onega

Lake Ladoga

Baltic Sea

MUSCOVY

Novgorod

Vyatka

Vyatka R.

PSKOV

Tver

Kazan

TVER

Moscow

Oka R.

KAZAN KHANATE

Dnieper R.

RYAZAN

URAL MOUNTAINS

LITHUANIA

Volga R.

Kyiv

Don R.

ASTRAKHAN KHANATE

POLAND

CRIMEAN KHANATE

Black Sea

Sea of Azov

200 km mi

Boundary in 1462	Boundary in 1521
Boundary in 1485	Boundary in 1260

could not have predicted that the child of Grand Prince Vasily would one day become "the classic Russian tyrant,"[4] as one modern historian puts it. Nor did they foresee that he would invade their lands in an attempt to create a Russian empire.

When Ivan was young, these neighboring lands included some large remnants of the Mongol Empire, which had encompassed most of Asia three centuries before. One of these "khanates" (so-called because their rulers were called khans) was the Crimea. It lay along the shores of the Black Sea directly south of Russia. Another was Kazan, situated east of Russian territory and north of the Caspian Sea. The Russians and Europeans called the inhabitants of the lands Tartars, their term for Mongols. Meanwhile, the western borders of Russia were defined by four Christian kingdoms: (from north to south) Finland, Livonia, Lithuania, and Poland.

Russia itself was a pie-shaped wedge of territory stretching from the Crimea in the south to the shores of the Arctic Ocean in the north. As a nation-state, Russia was a fairly new creation. Shattered by Mongol invasions, before the 1400s Russia had been a fragmented land. It had consisted of a group of more or less independent city-states, including Moscow, Novgorod, Vladimir, and Rostov.

Slowly but surely, however, a series of Muscovite rulers began to expand their power beyond Moscow. In so doing, they annexed neighboring city-states. Ivan's grandfather, Ivan III, absorbed Novgorod and its extensive territories, for example. Vasily III then added more lands to the growing Russian nation. Thus, young Ivan stood to inherit a large and still-growing kingdom with many populous cities and millions of acres of valuable farmland and forests.

Ivan's Early, Stable Years

Coming into that rightful inheritance proved a difficult and painful task for the young man, however. His father, Grand Prince Vasily, died of an infected sore in December 1533, when the boy was only three. In theory, Ivan was the new grand prince. But his tender age kept him from assuming actual power. So his mother became regent—chief adviser and administrator—until he was old enough to rule.

Elena herself was advised by, and in a sense shared power with, the Boyar Duma, a council of leading boyars. Elena also relied on the power and influence of a few strong male figures who were close to her. Her uncle, Mikhail Glinsky, for example, emerged as the leading noble and court official following Vasily's death. Soon, however, Elena took a lover, the handsome Prince

Ivan Obolensky. Worried that his own position in the court might be threatened, Glinsky tried to oust Obolensky. This prompted Elena to move against her uncle. She convinced the Duma that he was plotting to take full control of the government, and Glinsky ended up in chains in a dungeon.

MOSCOW AND THE KREMLIN IN THE 1500s

In 1553 an Englishman named Richard Chancelour visited Russia and met Ivan IV. Chancelour penned a description of his travels for the English government. This portion of the narrative describes the capital city of Moscow and the imposing Kremlin in which Ivan lived.

> Moscow itself is great. I take the whole town to be greater than London with the suburbs. But it is very rude and stands [in considerable disorder]. The houses are all of timber very dangerous for fire. There is a fair castle [the Kremlin], the walls of which are brick and very high. . . . The one side is ditched [i.e., has a moat] and on the other side runs a river. . . . The emperor [Ivan] lives in the castle, in which there are nine fair churches, and [in these live] religious men.

During Ivan's reign, the Kremlin was a formidable complex of palaces, churches, and other buildings.

Similar political intrigues involving nobles hungry for power continued regularly during the years Ivan was growing up. Elena and Obolensky wanted to shelter him from these and other nasty aspects of life. Hoping to keep him safe and stable, they raised him within the high stone walls of the Kremlin. This was the huge complex of palaces, churches, and other buildings in which the grand princes, their families, and their advisers lived and worked. The young prince was not only guarded closely but also lived in luxury, enjoying the finest foods, clothes, and toys.

Ivan also received the best education available from hired tutors. Early on the boy showed an avid interest in, perhaps even an obsession with, church rituals, sacred relics, and religious history. At the age of only six or seven he was memorizing long passages from the Bible. All who knew him saw that Ivan was unusually bright and perceptive, as well as passionate in expressing his opinions.

Ivan's keen intellect and powers of observation served him in another way as well. It became increasingly impossible for his elders to shelter him completely from the political struggles that were going on within the Kremlin. More and more the boy came to see most of the leading boyars as selfish, greedy men who cared little for him or his mother.

Unexpected Tragedy Strikes

Still, at least for a few years the young man did not worry about the future. His mother was always there to protect him. She also watched over her other son, Yury. Two years younger than Ivan, Yury had been born deaf, a disability that did not prevent the brothers from becoming playmates.

Then, tragedy struck. In April 1538 Elena, who was not yet 30, died suddenly. The exact cause of her death is unknown but was likely either a heart attack or deliberate poisoning. The fact that she was hurriedly buried in a Kremlin churchyard on the very day she died suggests that someone wanted to make sure there was no close examination of the body. As for motive, if it was indeed murder, Elena had always had enemies in the court. Also, many boyars resented and wanted to get rid of Obolensky. They knew that without Elena's support and protection, his power would collapse.

However Elena met her end, Ivan, then just eight years old, was devastated by the loss. In a letter written several years later, he recalled:

Thus by God's will it came to pass that our mother, the pious Elena, went from the earthly kingdom to the heavenly, and we and our brother

Yury were orphaned, being without parents and having no one to look after us, but trusting in God. We threw ourselves upon the mercy of the Most Pure Mother of God [the Virgin Mary] and the prayers of all the saints.[5]

Ivan's assertion that he and Yury had "no one to look after us" was in part a reference to the fall of Obolensky. Predictably, within days of Elena's passing the leading boyars arrested Obolensky and threw him into prison.

Orphaned and Neglected

With Elena and Obolensky gone, the most powerful member of the Boyar Duma, Vasily Shuisky, stepped forward and claimed power as Ivan's new regent. Unlike Obolensky, Shuisky had neither loyalty to nor sympathy for Ivan and Yury. Shuisky wanted power only for himself. Yet he realized that to keep and exercise that power he had to go through the motions of fulfilling the duties of official regent. To make his new position look even more legitimate, he forced Ivan's young cousin, Anastasia, to marry him. That made Shuisky a part of Ivan's family and placed the regent in line to become grand prince if anything happened to Ivan.

Meanwhile, Ivan and Yury's lives took a decided turn for the worse. Their well-being and comforts were of no concern to Shuisky, and the young princes were largely neglected. It appears that sometimes they even had to scrounge for food and proper clothing. "The Shuiskys treated us—myself and my brother—as though we were foreigners or the most wretched menials [servants]," Ivan later wrote.

> What sufferings I endured through lack of cloth-ing and from hunger! For in all things my will was not my own. . . . Everything was done contrary to my will, in a manner unbefitting my tender years. I recall one incident. I and my brother were playing together . . . and there was Shuisky, sitting on a bench, his elbows on my father's bed, his leg up in a chair, and he did not even incline his head toward us . . . nor did he show any humility toward us. Who can endure such arrogance?[6]

Ivan also found himself exploited for political purposes. On important public and religious holidays or when foreign dignitaries visited the court, Shuisky sent men to fetch the prince. The regent made sure Ivan was dressed in fine clothes. The boy then had to stand or sit in a prominent place during the ceremonies. Such false shows were intended to make it look as if the young prince was well treated and that Shuisky was acting strictly in Ivan's interests.

Not surprisingly, Ivan came to hate Shuisky, and indeed the whole Shuisky family, with a passion. A temporary measure of relief came when a Kremlin conspiracy brought another boyar, Ivan Belsky, to power as regent. But Belsky, a decent individual, made the mistake of allowing the deposed Shuisky to remain

Sitting on a throne, the young Ivan is surrounded by members of the Boyar Duma.

a free man. The treacherous Shuisky merely bided his time, waiting for an opportunity to strike back and reclaim his powerful position.

The Kingdom Threatened with Destruction

The opportunity Shuisky was hoping for came in July 1541. The ruler of the Crimean khanate, Khan Saip Guirey, launched a full-scale invasion of Russia. His enormous Tartar army pushed northward to a bend in the Oka River not far south of Moscow. There, an even larger army of Russians gathered, intent on repelling the invaders.

Back in Moscow, the frightened populace began preparing for a siege. The leading nobles decided that Ivan, then eleven, would prove useful in unifying the people. He was, after all, the figurehead of the government, even if he held no real power. They dressed the boy in royal robes and made a show of having him pray to images of the Virgin Mary in local cathedrals. "Be merciful to us, your children," Ivan recited in a prepared speech.

> Save us and all Christendom from the infidel
> Khan Saip Guirey, who is advancing against me
> and all the Russian lands with great confidence.
> Protect me and all the Russian lands, and be
> merciful, lest the infidels say: Where is their God
> in whom they put their trust?[7]

Fortunately for Ivan and his subjects, the Tartars never made it to Moscow. The forceful showing of Russian troops at the Oka made the khan think twice, and soon he ordered his troops to retreat back to the Crimea. For both Ivan and his new regent, Belsky, there was little time to celebrate, however. During the emergency, Shuisky had been given command of a large Russian army. He now used those troops to stage a coup and regain power.

Ivan's Mounting Fury

As in the past, Shuisky was not the only person who desired to exploit young Ivan and rule in his stead. So palace plots continued. One of the most ambitious schemers was Shuisky's cousin, Andrey. In May 1542 Vasily Shuisky died unexpectedly and Andrey seized the position of regent for the still underage Ivan.

Ivan found Andrey Shuisky to be even more cold and mean-spirited than the former regent. Andrey saw that Ivan was maturing rapidly. Soon, the regent reasoned, the boy might demand to begin exercising his legal authority as grand prince. This would clearly be a threat to Andrey's own authority. Hoping to avoid this turn of events, Andrey tried to isolate the prince from influential adults outside of the Shuisky family. That way, it would be more difficult for Ivan to form alliances against the regent.

Andrey was not always very subtle in executing this plan. In September 1542 a meeting of the Boyar Duma took place in a Kremlin dining hall. In addition to the Shuiskys and other nobles, Ivan was present, as was Metropolitan Makary. ("Metropolitan" was a title used by high-ranking bishops in the Russian Orthodox Church.) Fyodor Vorontsov, who had served Ivan's father and was one of the few nobles who remained loyal to the young prince, was also there. Without warning, several of the

Shuiskys attacked Vorontsov, tore his clothes, and beat him. Horrified, Ivan begged Makary to intervene. Makary did so, and this was the only reason that Vorontsov survived. He was thrown into prison, however, and could no longer communicate with Ivan.

Ivan did not react openly or rashly to this and other outrages perpetrated by Andrey Shuisky. Instead, the young man, who was a far more dangerous schemer than Andrey or anyone else suspected, concealed his mounting fury. Ivan waited patiently for his chance to settle the score with Andrey, the Shuiskys, and the boyars in general. In December 1543 Ivan felt ready to strike. He summoned Andrey Shuisky to his quarters. Thinking he had nothing to fear from a mere boy, the regent came alone. Suddenly Ivan ordered his personal

The Boyar Duma meets in the Kremlin in this painting. Andrey Shuisky and other boyars conspired against the young Ivan.

servants, who were still loyal to him, to seize Andrey. They carried the terrified regent to the Kremlin kennels. There, the uncouth young men who fed the royal hounds clubbed Andrey to death.

A Lesson About Murder

In one swift stroke, the thirteen-year-old Ivan had ended the official regency and seized his rightful position as grand prince of Russia. Moreover, he had accomplished this feat by ordering his first murder. Certainly he had witnessed or heard about many of the killings that routinely occurred as part of the power struggles within the Kremlin. But hearing about murder was one thing and actually commanding it was quite another. In a twisted way, the young man felt empowered by it. In the words of his modern biographer Robert Payne, he had learned that

> murder was an effective weapon, wonderfully satisfying in its speed and finality. He learned, too, that . . . when a man seizes power, it is incumbent on him to be cruel, for otherwise people will not grant him their [complete] respect. Ivan had learned his lesson. Henceforth he would be murderous whenever he pleased.[8]

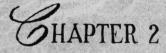

CHAPTER 2

TSAR, HUSBAND, AND REFORMER

Early in 1544, at the age of just thirteen, Ivan Vasilevich was in control of the Kremlin and the government. The once powerful Shuisky family had been removed from power, partly through the assassination of Andrey Shuisky by Ivan himself. This deed had made the young man a figure to be feared and respected. He now had two sturdy pillars on which to base his authority—his inherited title of grand prince and a reputation for ruthlessness.

However, the young man correctly judged that he was not yet ready to run the kingdom by himself. For the moment, he felt more

24

comfortable leaving the details of governing to more experienced adults. Of course, it was essential that these advisers be people he could trust. Therefore, he called on Fyodor Vorontsov, who had long given the boy both loyalty and friendship. After being attacked at court and saved by Makary, Vorontsov had been exiled. Ivan now canceled the exile, and Vorontsov returned to Moscow, where he and several members of his family assumed powerful positions in the Kremlin. Members of Ivan's mother's family, the Glinskys, soon rose to prominence as well.

As it turned out, bringing these two families together in the corridors of power was a recipe for trouble. The Vorontsovs and Glinskys did not get along and a keen rivalry developed. Eventually, the Glinskys prevailed. It is probable, though it remains unproven, that they manufactured evidence implicating some of the Vorontsovs in a supposed plot against Ivan. The accused men, including Fyodor, were beheaded.

While these intrigues were going on, Ivan spent much of his time doing whatever he wanted, a luxury he had been denied as a child. His brother, Yury, was still a close companion, and Ivan also gathered around himself a group of rowdy young men whom he thought of as friends. According to some sources of the era, the

This painting depicts Prince Ivan and his companions riding roughshod through the streets of Moscow.

young grand prince and his companions ran roughshod through Moscow. They robbed merchants and whipped innocent bystanders at will. It was also said that Ivan enjoyed tossing dogs off the Kremlin's battlements and watching them die in agony.

This largely irresponsible period of Ivan's life was relatively brief, however. When he was sixteen, the young man rather suddenly decided he was ready to become grand prince in more than just name. He also made it known that he was eager to get married. It quickly became clear to Ivan's advisers that he was going to be an energetic, ambitious ruler who had big plans for himself and the nation.

The Coronation

Ivan's first order of business in implementing these plans was to acquire official recognition of his position as grand prince. Per custom, he was to be crowned in a splendid public and religious ceremony. He and his advisers wanted it to be the biggest and most lavish coronation Russia had ever seen.

But these men wanted the ceremony to be about more than mere pomp and circumstance. Ivan saw the upcoming event as his golden opportunity to vault both himself and his country onto the world stage. And to do this he needed to be more than just a grand prince of Moscow. He needed to have a much more lofty title— such as "emperor." Then, he reasoned, he would have the prestige and authority to unite all of the Russian-speaking peoples, no matter where they dwelled. For instance, many Russian-speaking people lived in the region of the city of Kiev, then held by Poland and Lithuania. Numerous Russians also inhabited the khanates lying south and east of Russia. Ivan had designs on these lands and peoples. And he envisioned uniting all Russians in a great empire, with himself in complete charge, as emperor.

To achieve this grand vision, Ivan and his advisers realized they needed to create an imperial throne and royal court that people everywhere would recognize and respect. So for a model they looked to past examples, both outside and inside Russia. On the outside, there were the examples of the Roman and Byzantine empires. The Byzantine realm, centered in Greece, had only recently fallen, in 1453. It had been an outgrowth of western ancient Rome, which itself had fallen nearly a thousand years before. Though extinct, Rome and Byzantium remained the most prestigious and respected empires in history.

Even before Ivan was born, high-placed Russians dreamed of creating a Russian empire to rival those legendary realms. These men began calling Moscow the "Third Rome." Ivan now eagerly embraced this view. Roman and Byzantine emperors had used the title of Caesar, and he would call himself by the Russian version of this term—tsar (or czar). Some of Ivan's immediate predecessors had called themselves tsar as an informal, added title. But Ivan was the first to be officially crowned as tsar of "all Rus," or the emperor of Russians everywhere.

The gala ceremony took place on January 16, 1547. Following the Byzantine imperial model, the chief religious leader, in this case Makary, officiated. Before he placed the crown on Ivan's head, the young man made a speech, saying in part:

My father, Grand Prince Vasily . . . commanded
that I should ascend the grand princely throne
and be anointed and crowned with the Tsar's

Ivan is crowned in this scene from Sergei Eisenstein's 1945 film based on Ivan's life.

crown, according to our ancient customs. . . .
Therefore, our father [a reference to Makary],
you should bless my ascension to the throne and
pronounce me Grand Prince and Tsar crowned by
God. You should crown me now with the Tsar's
crown . . . according to God's will and the blessing of my father, Grand Prince Vasily.[9]

Smitten by Love

Soon after Ivan became emperor he decided that he
must also be married. He informed Makary that he

29

desired to take a bride, preferably a Russian-born girl. Happy at the prospect of the young man's tying the knot and raising a family, Makary suggested the daughter of a leading boyar who had recently died. Her name was Anastasia Zakharina.

Anastasia was beautiful, witty, even-tempered, and a joy to be with. She was also deeply religious. For the new tsar, who was fascinated by church customs and lore, that alone made her very attractive as a potential mate. Needless to say, Ivan approved of Makary's choice. The wedding took place on February 3, 1547, less than three weeks after the coronation. After the ceremony, the bride and groom spent most of the day praying at local monasteries.

Ivan was clearly smitten with his new bride and treated her with the utmost respect. A number of people close to the royal family claimed that she

This illustration depicts the wedding of Ivan and Anastasia Zakharina in February 1547, less than three weeks after Ivan was crowned tsar.

had a sort of calming effect on him. In fact, some were convinced that Anastasia's influence, coupled with that of Makary, would induce the young man to settle down to a quiet life.

But this was not to be. When he was in his wife's company, Ivan was courteous, restrained, even genteel. When she was not around, however, he often displayed fits of temper and cruelty. More and more he seemed paranoid that underlings were plotting against him. And he showed little patience with even the simplest expressions of discontent by his subjects.

Not long after his wedding, for instance, while riding in the countryside Ivan encountered a group of elders from the town of Pskov. They presented him with a petition that called for the removal of the local governor, who, the elders explained, was corrupt and abusive. Instead of showing concern and promising to look into the matter, the tsar flew into a rage. He forced the men to strip naked and lie in the snow. Then he and his guards set their beards on fire.

Disaster and Divine Wrath

It is possible that Ivan would have gone on to kill the men from Pskov. They were saved, however, when a messenger arrived from Moscow. He informed the tsar that the enormous bell in the city's biggest cathedral had fallen. Ivan immediately galloped off to deal with the crisis. This was only one of many urban emergencies the young ruler was forced to deal with during his reign.

Many of these disasters were fire related. At the time, Moscow was built almost entirely of wood and the houses and shops were crowded closely together. Moreover, people lit their dwellings with candles and torches and used open hearths for cooking and heating. Such practices greatly raised the risk of fires. Not surprisingly, every year numerous small and moderate-sized blazes broke out.

A much larger fire broke out in June of the year of Ivan's coronation and marriage. It began in a church on a crowded street in the heart of the city and spread quickly. Then the wind changed direction and carried the flames over the Kremlin walls. Several of the magnificent churches inside were destroyed. Meanwhile, as Robert Payne memorably phrases it:

Moscow was transformed into a great crackling bonfire under a black cloud of smoke which was torn into ribbons by the strong winds. Flames fed on flames; stone buildings crumbled or exploded;

wooden houses became puffs of smoke; people with smoke-blackened faces wandered desolately through fields of ashes.[10]

When the fire was finally put out, the citizens of Moscow, including the tsar himself, were stunned by the immensity of the disaster. Thousands of people had died, tens of thousands were homeless, and much of the city lay in ruins. The tsar convened a meeting of the Boyar Duma to deal with the crisis. There he heard some of the theories for what had caused the fire. Many Muscovites were convinced the culprits were *serdechniki* (ghouls, zombies, or evil spirits). Others said that the Glinskys had purposely started the fire. Large numbers of people distrusted that family, partly because of its foreign origins, and believed some of its members wanted to destroy Russia.

In contrast, the deeply religious and superstitious Ivan came to see the great fire as a punishment sent by God. In fact, he had developed an obsession with and fear of sin and divine wrath. In some twisted way, perhaps stemming from personal guilt, it seemed to go hand in hand with his repeated bouts of brutality. In a remarkable speech made in hopes of absolving his sins, Ivan is reported to have said:

It was beyond my understanding that God was inflicting great punishments on me, and therefore I did not repent my sins. . . . God punished me for my sins with floods and plague, and even then I did not repent. Then God sent great fires and terror entered my soul, and my bones trembled. . . . I was filled with great spiritual emotion.[11]

Administrative and Legal Reforms

To some degree at least, Ivan's attitude regarding divine punishment was shaped by a brilliant and outspoken priest. His name was Sylvester and he hailed from Novgorod, north of Moscow. In the words of noted Russian scholar Andrei Pavlov, Sylvester "possessed enormous spiritual authority and he perhaps exerted greater influence on Tsar Ivan than any other member of the clergy."[12] Ivan initially had great respect for this priest. As a result, Sylvester was able to get away with saying things to the tsar that no one else could. He urged Ivan to be pious and to rule with justice and kindness. And he warned the ruler that God was always watching and would severely punish him for any sins.

Partly because he had the tsar's trust, Sylvester also played a major role in helping Ivan plan various reforms during the early years of his reign. Another major contributor to the planning was a prominent noble and the country's leading diplomat, Aleksey Adashev. It had become clear to all Russian leaders, including Ivan, that reforms were badly needed. The governmental, legal, and military institutions then in place were outdated. They had been designed for administering separate city-states of minimal extent, not a united, sprawling nation with millions of inhabitants. Also, much corruption had set in at all levels during the years of boyar rule.

One of the biggest reforms of Ivan's reign was the creation of chancelleries, or organized departments, in

The priest, Sylvester, seen here bowing to Ivan IV in Eisenstein's film, had a powerful influence over the Tsar.

the government. Before, the system was haphazard and inefficient. Groups of high-placed men simply carried out the orders of a ruler or the Duma. Now, there were specialized departments, each with a professional administrator. One chancellery maintained the palace. Another oversaw diplomacy, and others dealt with the treasury, the military, and so on.

In addition, in June 1550 Ivan introduced significant reforms in the nation's law code, the *Sudebnik*. One important aspect of the new code was a system of punishments for public officials who abused their powers. Another law abolished tax exemptions that had existed for the richest landowners.

Other Reforms

Among the other reforms Ivan instituted in his early reign were several relating to the country's military. The tsar realized that to fulfill his ambition to expand Russia's borders he would need a reliable, flexible army. Before his reforms, most of the soldiers were cavalrymen (mounted fighters) belonging to the upper classes. Also, many rich men were able to avoid military service altogether. The new system regularized military service so that all landowners had to contribute a certain number of cavalrymen for the army. Also, a special unit of infantrymen (foot soldiers) was created. They were armed with an early type of musket, a forerunner of the rifle.

In addition, Sylvester convinced the tsar to issue the *Domostroy*, a household code of conduct. Sylvester likely wrote parts of it himself. The document not only gave specific advice on food preparation and clothes making but also laid down rules of proper conduct among family

THE ROLE OF WOMEN

The *Domostroy* a guide to household conduct introduced during Ivan's reign, contained a section defining the role and duties of women. It said in part:

In all affairs of everyday life, the wife is to take counsel with [i.e., follow the orders of] her husband, and to ask him if he needs anything. . . . Let her put on the best garment, if she receives a guest. . . . By all means let her abstain from drinking liquor, for a drunk man is bad enough, but a drunk woman has no place in the world. A woman ought to talk with her lady friends of handiwork and housekeeping. . . . Let not a woman rail at anyone, nor gossip about others. If she should be asked something about a person, let her answer, "I know nothing about it, and have heard nothing of it. I do not inquire about things that do not concern me."

members and servants. For example, when delivering a message to a neighbor's house, a servant should bow before the holy images, give his master's respects, and tell his message. While doing so, let him not put his finger in his nose, nor cough, nor clean his nose . . . nor spit. If he absolutely must do so, let him step aside. He must stand straight and not look to either side when reporting the message.[13]

The *Domostroy* was widely read among the nobles and other literate Russians. But these groups were numerically small. Most people were not literate. Also, the printing press had not yet reached Russia, so only a few hundred handmade copies of the text were available.

These and other reforms introduced in Ivan's early reign do not seem very progressive to modern eyes. After all, most new institutions and laws benefited either the government or the nobles. The lives and rights of common people did not change much. But for their time, these changes were major. Moreover, they made the government and army much more efficient. This was essential for the maintenance of a strong monarchy and an aggressive foreign policy, Ivan's two highest priorities.

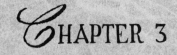

CHAPTER 3

IVAN ATTEMPTS TO BUILD AN EMPIRE

By becoming tsar, Ivan had made himself an emperor. But at the
time of his coronation he had no empire. The young ruler dreamed of
expanding Russia's borders eastward, southward, and westward. Such
conquests would bring many Russian-speaking people, as well as
numerous non-Russians, into the realm. Ivan also saw it as his duty to
spread the Russian Orthodox brand of Christianity. People of other
faiths, whom he called infidels, must be converted or destroyed.
During the planning stages of one campaign, he told his wife,
Anastasia:

It is my wish and desire to make war against the infidels, placing my trust in Almighty God, who loves mankind. I desire to wage war on behalf of the Orthodox faith and the holy churches, not only unto the shedding of my blood, but even unto death, for it is sweet to die for the Orthodox faith. . . . Thus did the [Christian] martyrs undergo their sufferings, and so did the apostles [of Jesus], and the former Tsars who lived in fear of God. . . . God gave them a place in Heaven because they were God-fearing and because they suffered for the sake of Orthodoxy.[14]

Greed for land and power and religious zeal were not the only motives driving Ivan's aggressive foreign policy, however. Part of his strategy was defensive in nature. Russia had long been and continued to be threatened by the Tartar khanates lying to the south and east. In addition to the Crimea and Kazan, there was Astrakhan, situated on the shores of the Caspian Sea. All three kingdoms regularly sent large raiding parties into southern Russia. The intruders burned villages, stole gold and other valuables, and kidnapped Russian citizens. These unfortunate individuals became slaves to the khans or were sold in distant slave markets.

IVAN THE TERRIBLE

For all of these reasons, Ivan waged a long series of wars between 1552 and the late 1570s. Many thousands of people, both Russian and non-Russian, were killed. Death also pervaded the tsar's private life in this period. Several of those closest to him passed away, leaving him grief-stricken and more angry than ever.

Ivan Attacks the Tartars

Anger was certainly one motivation for Ivan's campaigns against Kazan. The Tartars of that kingdom had been a thorn in Russia's side for generations. And the young tsar was determined to remove it. At one point, he told his assembled nobles and troops:

An illustration from a sixteenth-century manuscript shows Ivan (right foreground) leading a charge against the Tartars of Kazan.

Strive [in the coming struggle] on behalf of our brothers, those Orthodox Christians who have been made captive for many years without reason and who have suffered terribly at the hands of the infidels of Kazan. . . . Better that I die here than live to see Christ blasphemed and the Christians . . . suffering at the hands of the heathen Tartars of Kazan![15]

The first major Russian foray into the khanate of Kazan began early in 1551. Ivan led an army into Tartar territory and captured several small towns. In the process, Ivan's troops liberated tens of thousands of Russians who had been captured in Tartar raids. Some were found bound in cellars and holes in the ground, where their slave masters had hidden them. Ivan also built a fortress only a few miles from the khanate's capital, also called Kazan.

The following year, Ivan launched a larger attack on Kazan. His army besieged the capital from August through October. One of the highlights of the operation was the building of a giant wooden siege tower. It stood 42 feet (12.8m) high, several feet taller than the city's walls. Ivan placed more than 50 cannons in the tower and manned them with his most skilled gunners. The Russians dragged the tower to Kazan's walls and, as Payne describes it:

IVAN THE TERRIBLE

At dawn there was a thunderous roar as the guns fired directly into the city, causing fearful damage and killing vast numbers of women and children. The Tartar soldiers behind the Khan's gate quickly dug trenches to put up earthworks, but the presence of the huge tower bristling with guns was a constant reminder of the massive power of the invaders.[16]

Before the final attack on the city, Ivan spoke to his troops. To build up their morale, he made them many promises. Those who suffered in the assault, he said, would receive glory both on Earth and in heaven. Their names would be repeated and revered in church services. "Should you die," he added, "I shall take care of your wives and children and pay your creditors."[17]

It is unknown whether the tsar actually intended to keep these promises. But it is certain that they had the desired effect. His men fought hard and captured Kazan. Among the heroes of the siege was a young noble named Andrey Kurbsky. The tsar congratulated Kurbsky and other officers. And soon afterward they congratulated him. For in the same month that Kazan fell, Ivan's wife, Anastasia, gave birth to a baby boy, whom they named Dmitry.

Tartar nobles bow their heads to the ground in a gesture of surrender to Ivan.

Relations with the West

Following the conquest of Kazan, Ivan turned his attention to the khanate of Astrakhan, lying farther south. The Russians overran it in 1554. Of the former Mongol lands that Ivan felt rightfully belonged to Russia, that left only the Crimean khanate. This kingdom was stronger than the others, however. Attacking it was also more dangerous because of what lay beyond it. The opposite shores of the Black Sea were controlled by the Ottoman Turks, who had conquered the Byzantine Empire in the 1400s. Even if Ivan managed to overrun the Crimea, he would then share a border with the formidable Turks. Nevertheless, the Russians did go on the attack against the Crimean khanate. A series of largely indecisive battles were fought along Russia's southern flanks in the late 1550s.

During these same years, Ivan also wisely looked beyond the lands situated on Russia's western borders— Lithuania and Livonia. He dreamed of defeating these lands. Of the European kingdoms that lay still farther west, he had heard that England and several of its neighbors were powerful and prosperous. It occurred to him that making friends with these countries might create new allies against his enemies. Such alliances would also help Russia by giving it access to rich new trade markets. In addition, the Russians might learn a great deal from European doctors, artists, teachers, and engineers.

In the late 1540s and on into the 1550s, therefore, Ivan eagerly nurtured contacts with the West. At one point, his agents managed to interest several hundred European doctors, artists, and others to come to Russia. But when they reached Livonia, the local authorities would not allow them to pass. Not surprisingly, this further fueled Ivan's desire to invade and conquer Livonia when he felt the time was right.

In the meantime, relations between Russia and England were more fruitful. An English explorer,

IVAN ATTEMPTS TO BUILD AN EMPIRE

Richard Chancelour, sailed into the White Sea, on Russia's northwestern flank, in 1553. Russian authorities welcomed him and escorted him to Moscow to meet the tsar. The two men got along well. Chancelour later penned an account of his visit, which contains a vivid description of Ivan and his royal court:

> I came into the council chamber, where sat the [tsar] himself with his nobles, which were a fair company. . . . [Ivan] sat much higher than any of his nobles in a chair gilded [with gold], and in a long garment of beaten gold, with an imperial crown upon his head, and a staff of crystal and gold in his right hand. . . . He bade me welcome and inquired of me the health of the king, my master.[18]

In fact, the meetings between Ivan and Chancelour went so well that in 1555, during the Englishman's second visit to Russia, he and Ivan signed an agreement. The tsar promised to allow the English to trade all they wanted without paying any duties. Also, the Russian government would pay the English for any losses they suffered at the hands of pirates while in Russian territory.

In addition, Ivan proposed to send a Russian ambassador to England to meet the king and queen of that

In 1555 Ivan discusses the terms of a trade agreement with English diplomats.

land. This honor fell on a well-to-do town official and merchant named Osip Nepea. Nepea reached London in 1557. A serious, courteous individual, he made a good impression on the English leaders. They expressed their desire to develop a closer relationship with his distant country and its young tsar.

The Livonian War

Less than a year after the English welcomed Nepea, Ivan was on the offensive again. This time the target was Livonia, which consisted of a loose confederation of five city-states lying along the southern shores of the Baltic Sea. Ivan wanted access to that waterway and the considerable seagoing trade it supported. This would allow the Russians easier access to the European markets beyond. It would also bring valuable, strategically placed lands into the growing Russian empire.

The tsar tried to justify his claim to Livonia in a letter to Sigismund II Augustus, king of Poland: "God

An official from a town in Livonia surrenders to Ivan and his men.

knows, and so do all the rulers and all the people, to whom Livonia rightfully belongs. From the time of our ancestors until this day, Livonia has always belonged to us."[19] The Polish king disagreed. He had his own disputes with the Livonians. But he did not want to see them fall to Ivan because then it would be easier for the Russians to attack Poland.

At first, the Livonian strongholds fell to Ivan like dominoes. In 1558 the Russians captured or accepted the surrender of twenty major towns in Livonia. These included the largest and most prosperous—Dorpat, which fell without a fight. Its leaders opened their gates to the invaders after receiving assurances from a Russian general that they would be well treated. He kept his word.

Once again Andrey Kurbsky played a key role in the campaign. In 1559 Ivan dispatched Kurbsky to Dorpat to take charge of the war. Displaying his usual skill and daring as a soldier, as well as his loyalty to the tsar, Kurbsky scored several victories.

In time, however, the tide of the Livonian War began to change. The rulers of Sweden and Denmark became worried about Russian expansion and sent troops to aid the Livionians. Then, in 1561, those Livonian cities that had not yet fallen made a desperate move to save themselves from Russian domination. They voluntarily submitted to Polish rule. As a result, the following year Ivan found himself at war with Poland. In the years to come, the later phases of the Livonian War would increasingly drain Russia's human and material resources.

Sickness and Tragedy

The turbulent period in which Ivan began expanding Russia's borders was also often stormy for him personally. One of the most distressing incidents occurred in March 1553 when he suddenly fell ill with a high fever and could not leave his bed. The exact identity of the illness is unknown, but some evidence suggests that he had a severe bout of pneumonia.

Whatever the nature of the illness, the tsar was convinced he was dying and addressed himself to the royal succession. He urged his leading boyars to swear allegiance to his infant son, Dmitry. But they were reluctant to do so. This was partly because they did not like the prospect of another long regency, with its inevitable uncertainties and rivalries among the nobles. Ivan kept insisting, however. He told them:

> I hold the Cross to you, and I command you to serve my son Dmitry. . . . I cannot speak much

more. You have forgotten your oaths [made earlier to the Tsar] because you do not want to serve me and my children. . . . Those who refuse to serve a Tsar in swaddling clothes would not wish to serve him when he grows up. If you reject me, then let it be on your souls![20]

Eventually, the boyars gave in and swore their allegiance to baby Dmitry. But in a sense it was too late. To everyone's surprise, the tsar's condition improved and he soon fully recovered. Moreover, he was not about to forget what he viewed as a despicable display of disloyalty. Ivan had long been overly distrustful of people and paranoid that they were plotting against him. This incident only served to magnify these anxious feelings.

Soon after, a series of tragedies occurred, each of which plunged the young tsar into despair and further hardened his heart. In June 1553, only a few months after he had recovered from his illness, baby Dmitry died. Three years later, Ivan and Anastasia had a daughter, Evdokia, but the child died in 1558 at age two. Then, in 1560, Anastasia died as well. And in 1563 both Ivan's brother, Yury, and his old friend Makary passed away.

IVAN ATTEMPTS TO BUILD AN EMPIRE

Kurbsky's Flight

For the emotionally unstable Ivan, all of these losses proved to be wounds that never seemed to heal. More and more, he vented his mounting frustrations on innocent people. After news of a military defeat on the Livonian front reached him in 1564, he flew into a rage and unfairly laid the blame on several of his leading boyars. These included administrators and army officers who had long been loyal and valuable to him. The tsar's henchmen murdered two of these men—Mikhail Repnin and Yury Kashin—while they were praying in church.

IVAN AND KURBSKY BATTLE WITH PENS

In the letters exchanged between the tsar and his former commander Andrey Kurbsky, the two men vented their fury. Kurbsky accused Ivan of murder, lying, and other crimes. "You have transformed the tsardom of Russia into a fortress in hell by . . . suppressing freedom," Kurbsky wrote. Ivan responded in part by accusing the other man of crimes he had not committed, including killing the tsar's wife, Anastasia (who died of natural causes). "You began to act against me and betray me," Ivan charged. "And so I set myself against you with greater severity. I wanted you to submit to my will, and because of this—how you defiled and outraged the sanctity of the Lord!"

These violent acts sickened and angered another high-ranking Russian, the war hero Andrey Kurbsky. In April 1564 he became convinced that he would be Ivan's next victim, so he fled in the middle of the night. Leaving behind all of his possessions, he made his way to Lithuania, where Ivan's enemies welcomed him and gave him safe refuge.

Kurbsky decided that the tsar needed to be told how he was harming his country and its people. Between 1564 and 1579, the two men exchanged a series of long letters. In them, Kurbsky denounced Ivan's crimes and urged him to reform himself. In response, the tsar defended his actions, saying that God had given him the right to seek out and destroy evil within the realm. Kurbsky also wrote a firsthand account of Ivan's reign called the *History of the Grand Prince of Moscow*.

These writings have survived. They bear witness to a ruler who began with good intentions but steadily descended into tyranny. Indeed, to Kurbsky's horror, the periodic brutalities that had marred the early years of Ivan's reign paled in comparison to what came later. Less than a year after Kurbsky's escape, the tsar's infamous reign of terror began.

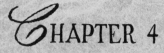

CHAPTER 4

THE TSAR ADOPTS RULE BY TERROR

From his safe vantage in Lithuania, where he had fled, Andrey Kurbsky watched events unfold in his native land. And he became very disturbed. Ivan's murders of high-ranking Russians in 1564 proved to be an ominous prelude to far worse bloodletting. In the months and years that followed, in fact, the tsar plunged the country into a virtual reign of terror. Tens of thousands of innocent people lost their lives. And almost everyone lived in a constant state of fear.

God's Agent of Death?

It was Ivan's cruelty and brutality during these years that earned him the nickname "the Terrible." And since that time historians, psychologists, and ordinary observers have wondered about and debated the tsar's motivations. Why did he become more and more paranoid, ruthless, and savage as he grew older? Was he mentally ill? Was he evil? Or might his crimes be explained in other ways?

Modern historians and mental health experts have proposed a number of different theories to explain the causes of Ivan's fear, rage, and violent nature. Some suggest that Ivan suffered from a now well-known form of mental illness that makes a person feel constantly persecuted. The person believes that nearly everyone is out to get him or

In this movie still, Tsar Ivan witnesses the execution of one of his enemies.

55

her. Many victims of this condition react by withdrawing from society and avoiding people. In Ivan's case, by contrast, he was a national leader with immense power at his disposal. His reaction may have been to use that power to strike back at his mostly imaginary enemies. The tsar also watched his beloved wife, brother, son, and several others close to him die. His deluded mind may have seen these deaths not as normal losses but as part of a larger conspiracy against him.

One of the more intriguing and well-supported theories for Ivan's twisted mind and acts involves his religious views. A number of scholars now believe that Ivan was a religious fanatic who allowed his extreme views to cloud his judgment. These scholars point out that many of the brutal punishments Ivan inflicted followed a set pattern. They closely resembled the sufferings that medieval Christians thought went on in hell. These included burning, roasting alive, having limbs cut off, and being eaten by wild animals.

In this view, Ivan saw himself as God's "angel of death" on Earth. In his demented mind, God had given him the task of punishing wicked and guilty people. It was, he believed, part of a worldwide cleansing of sin. The Book of Revelation, in the Bible, claimed that this cleansing would immediately precede the second coming of Jesus Christ. As

Andrei Pavlov puts it, "The growth of evil and lawlessness in Russia . . . indicated to Ivan that the 'last days' were indeed approaching and that it was his sacred duty to punish the wicked ahead of the Last Judgment."[21]

A Strange Departure

Whatever twisted motives or mental conditions lay behind Ivan's brutal acts, one thing is certain. Once his violent behavior began, it steadily got worse. He arrested, tortured, and killed more and more people each year. In this way, he increasingly abused his great powers as tsar. And thereby he fulfilled the famous adage describing almost all dictators and tyrants in history: Absolute power corrupts absolutely.

The beginning of the most corrupt phase of Ivan's rule began late in 1564. In November, for reasons no one at the time could comprehend, the tsar removed many gold crosses and other holy artifacts from local churches. He ordered these items loaded onto carts. Ivan also had his servants pack many of his clothes and other personal belongings. Some people guessed that he was going to visit some shrines or monasteries in the countryside, as he often did.

On December 3, however, the tsar revealed that this would not be the usual religious pilgrimage. He gathered

In 1565 Ivan began a campaign of purges against many boyars and those who associated with them.

together the country's leading clergymen, nobles, and merchants. He told them that he was leaving Moscow to set up residence in the small town of Alexandrova Sloboda, about 60 miles (96.56km) from the capital. Exactly why he was doing this, he did not say.

After the tsar left, there was a great deal of discussion and worry. "Never before," Robert Payne writes, had Ivan "left Moscow burdened with so many holy images or by so much gold plate from his treasury." The boyars, priests, and others had "an uneasy feeling that some strange silent drama was being performed." They knew that Ivan "was not the kind of person who would simply leave Moscow and vanish from sight. He was one of those who would make their presence felt even when they were far away."[22]

Two Ominous Letters

A month went by before Ivan began to make his real intentions clear. In January 1565 he sent two letters to Metropolitan Afanasy, who had taken Makary's place as Russia's spiritual leader. One letter was addressed to the boyars and other prominent courtiers. The tsar accused them of conspiring against him. They were traitors, he said, and thieves who had stolen money from the state treasury. They were also cowards who had failed to fight hard enough for him on the battlefields of Livonia and elsewhere.

The second letter from Ivan was addressed to the people of Moscow. The tsar made it clear that he was not angry with the common people. It was their masters, the boyars, who were the scoundrels, he said. Afanasy and others saw quite clearly that Ivan was attempting to drive a wedge between the nobles and common people. Without popular support, the boyars would be less able to resist the punishments the tsar was planning for them. Just as he had hoped, the letter caused much unrest among the people. One contemporary account claims that a delegation of townspeople told Afanasy:

Woe on us who have sinned before God and angered the Tsar by our many wrongdoings

59

against him. To whom shall we turn now, and who will save us from the attacks of foreigners? How can the sheep live without a shepherd? How can we endure without a Tsar?[23]

Part of Ivan's intention in writing these letters was to inject fear and confusion into the ranks of the nobles. And in this he succeeded masterfully. Adding to their anxiety was the fact that the tsar had gathered large numbers of troops in Alexandrova Sloboda. In fact, he was turning the town into an armed camp. The boyars feared that these troops might be used against Moscow. So the leading nobles drew up a petition that begged Ivan to return and rule them as he had before:

With grave reluctance and sorrow in our hearts, we have learned from our Great Lord, who merits every praise, that he is displeased with us and especially that he is abandoning the Tsardom and us. We are but poor . . . sheep without a shepherd, and the wolves, our enemies, surround us. We therefore request and beg him to see fit to change his mind. . . . Should the Tsar agree to hear our petition, we shall gladly submit ourselves to his rule.[24]

The Separate Kingdom

The petitioners submitted their plea to the tsar in Alexandrova Sloboda. There, after further denouncing the boyars, he hit them with another bombshell. Ivan announced that he would return to Moscow and rule from that city only when he saw fit. Furthermore, he would do so only on two conditions, which the boyars must formally accept. First, he would create a separate kingdom within Russia's borders. It would be called the *Oprichnina*, from the word *oprich*, meaning "apart" or "separate." This new subunit of the country would have its own administrators, police, and judges, who would report directly to the tsar. And only those nobles whom

Ivan garrisoned a large number of troops in Alexandrova Slobda (pictured), turning the town into an armed camp.

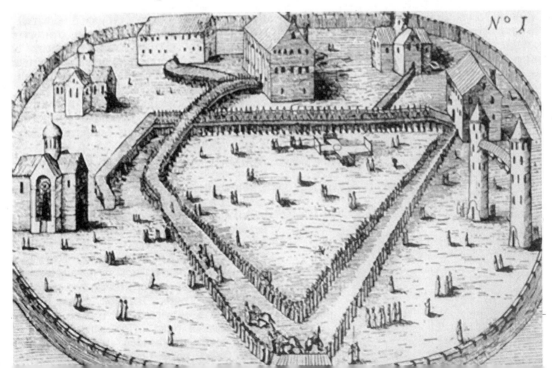

Ivan trusted would be allowed to live in the *Oprichnina*. Other boyars would run the other sections of the country. But they would still be expected to do his bidding.

The boyars thought that this proposed new administrative arrangement was strange. But many of them felt it was something they could live with. The second condition Ivan imposed for accepting the petition was much more ominous. From his kingdom within a kingdom, the tsar declared, he would mete out justice on wrongdoers as he saw fit. He would decide who was or was not a traitor or other criminal. And he would retain the unquestioned right to arrest and execute such people at any time and then confiscate their property.

The leading boyars immediately accepted Ivan's two conditions. Of course, they had no other choice, since they knew that the tsar could at any moment use the army or the common people against them. About a month later, in February, Ivan kept his part of the bargain by returning to Moscow. But he confined himself to one small section of the city and an even smaller corner of the Kremlin. These areas were to be part of the *Oprichnina*. About twenty selected towns and some scattered stretches of farmland and forests would also be included in the separate kingdom. The rest of the Kremlin, the city of Moscow, and the Russian

The executioner on the right rolls up his sleeves as he prepares to decapitate a boyar in front of Ivan (sitting, foreground).

countryside would be collectively designated the *zemshchina*, an inferior region.

Some of the boyars hoped that this bizarre division of the country and Ivan's threats to kill traitors at will were a passing phase. But they were wrong. Almost immediately the arrests and executions began. The tsar accused Alexander Gorbaty-Shuisky, a hero of the Kazan campaigns, of treason. The man's seventeen-year-old son was arrested on the same charge. Although the charges were completely false, father and son were beheaded without a trial. Soon afterward, another boyar, Peter Gorensky, was arrested. A longtime loyal supporter and friend of the tsar, he was also wrongly charged with treason. Gorensky fled. But Ivan's henchmen caught up with him, impaled him on a big spike, and hanged all the relatives and servants who were with him.

The Tsar Adopts rule by Terror

Ivan's Dark Army

The henchmen who killed Gorensky and many others at Ivan's commands were members of his dreaded new order, the *oprichniki*. These black-robed assassins at first numbered about 1,000. But their ranks soon swelled to more than 6,000, more than enough to terrorize the entire country. They were a sort of dark army with no sense of honor or justice. Loyal not to Russia but to the tsar himself, they committed whatever brutal acts he ordered without question. In fact, they swore an oath of loyalty to him, part of which read:

> I swear to be loyal to my lord the Tsar and to his kingdom [the *Oprichnina*] . . . and I swear not to be silent about any evils I know of, those that I have heard or will hear about, which are [committed] by this or that person against the Tsar. . . . I also swear on oath that I shall not eat or drink or have any dealings with, or have anything in common with, anyone from the *zemshchina*. On this I kiss the cross [of Jesus].[25]

The *oprichniki* were recruited mostly from small towns and farms across Russia. They underwent extensive interviews. If they had any sort of relationship with boyars whom Ivan distrusted, they were rejected. Once accepted into the dark army, they received valuable rewards for their service. Among these were prosperous estates that the tsar snatched from various nobles.

The evicted boyars and their families were forced to leave their estates with only the clothes on their backs and to march hundreds of miles to "new estates." These were usually worthless wastelands located far from civilized areas. Moreover, Ivan forbade anyone from

Riding on horseback, Ivan is flanked by his oprichniki, the black-robed assassins who carried out the tsar's will.

helping these refugees. A decree declared that a person who did help them "shall be executed without mercy and his body not buried, but left for the birds, the dogs, and wild animals."[26]

One of the more perverse aspects of the *oprichniki* was the way Ivan masked their barbarity in respectable religious ritual. He often treated them like a combination of monk and knight. When quartered in their main base at Alexandrova Sloboda, they rose early each morning and attended church services for hours. The tsar himself presided over these ceremonies. The *oprichniki* were allowed to call him "brother," and he addressed each of them the same way. Later they had a hearty breakfast and said more prayers.

Obsessed with Torture

After all of this pious show, Ivan and his so-called brothers proceeded to the local dungeons to torture people. Some witnesses claimed he became cheerful and animated at the prospect of watching or taking part in these grisly sessions. In fact, as Payne points out:

Torture, which had always fascinated him, now obsessed him. He was continually inventing new and more excruciating forms of torture, while he filled the emptiness of his life with imaginary enemies, imaginary plots, and imaginary crimes.[27]

Sometimes Ivan used torture to try to get people to confess to crimes they had not committed. Other times he was after their gold or other valuables. But just as often he tortured people because he believed it was their just punishment for interfering with or plotting against the tsar and God. He was firmly convinced that such punishments were God's will and therefore acceptable. In his history of Ivan's reign, Andrey Kurbsky described the plight of one noble, Ivan Sheremetev, who had dared to disagree with the ruler about his war policies:

> His torture chamber was a terribly cramped cell with a rough earthen floor. Heavy chains were fastened round his neck and his arms and legs, while a thick iron hoop girdled his loins [genital area] with ten weights of iron hanging from it. The Tsar came to talk to him while he lay prostrate [flat] on the rough floor, wearing his heavy chains, half-alive and scarcely breathing.[28]

Many others met similar fates in the months and years that followed. Others were simply murdered

THE TSAR ADOPTS RULE BY TERROR

IVAN INTERROGATES A PRISONER

Both before and after the onset of his reign of terror in 1565, Ivan frequently took part in sessions of torture and questioning. In this excerpt from Andrey Kurbsky's history of Ivan's reign, the tsar demands that a shackled and very stubborn boyar reveal where he has hidden his treasure.

"Tell me, for I know you are very rich. Nevertheless, I have failed to find in your treasure house what I expected to find."

"They lie hidden where no one can find them."

"You must tell me. Otherwise I shall add torture to torture."

"Do as you wish. I am near the end of my journey."

"I insist that you tell me about your treasure."

"I have already told you that even if I told you where they were, you would not be able to make use of them. The hands of the poor and the needy have removed them to the heavenly treasure house, to my Christ."

Ivan watches as a prisoner is roasted alive on a spit.

outright. Meanwhile, the *oprichniki* routinely rounded up the victims' wives, children, servants, and friends. These so-called accomplices were killed, too, often after being tortured and raped by their black-robed captors. All of Russia was gripped by fear, and many wondered when the terror would end. They had no way of knowing that it was going to get worse—much worse—before it got better.

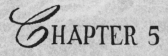

CHAPTER 5

IVAN MASSACRES HIS OWN PEOPLE

hroughout the remainder of the year 1565 and on into the following year, Ivan's reign of terror continued. During the early phases of the terror, the tsar and his henchmen, the *oprichniki*, mostly singled out individuals or small groups of people. Ivan and an assistant would compile a death list. The names on the list typically included various nobles that the tsar suspected of treason. Also listed, however, were servants, merchants, farmers, and others who had associated with these nobles.

The fearsome black-clad riders also murdered Russian citizens at random. In this case, the victims were not suspected of any crime but died at the whim of the *oprich-niki*, whom the tsar had given a virtual license to kill. Like Ivan, they also enjoyed killing and inflicting pain and suffering. A surviving, riveting eyewitness account of these assassins at work was penned by two assassins named Taube and Kruse. "None of the victims knew what crime they had committed," they later recalled,

or when he would die, or whether he had been condemned to death. Thus, each man went unsuspectingly to work, to the courts and the offices, and suddenly the *oprichniki* would descend upon him, strangle him or cut him to pieces in the street, at the gates, or in the market-places, although he was

As Ivan's reign of terror intensified, he began to engage in large-scale massacres, ordering his oprichniki *to storm entire towns.*

IVAN MASSACRES HIS OWN PEOPLE

quite innocent. The bodies were left to lie on the ground and no one was permitted to bury them. The marketplaces and the streets were so filled with corpses that the people, and the foreigners too, could not go about their work, not only because they were afraid, but also because of the unbearable stench.[29]

Over time, however, simple lists of a few dozen individuals, along with some random murders, were not enough for Ivan. He began to resort to large-scale massacres. These culminated in attacks on entire towns, including one of Russia's largest cities. The specific reasons for this frightening expansion of the terror are unknown. Perhaps the tsar came to believe the delusion that entire local populations were plotting against him. Or maybe he felt that he needed to set a larger and more horrific example for any would-be traitors.

Philipp Defies the Tsar

There was another ominous sign that Ivan's reign of terror was breaking new ground. For the first time he went after the metropolitan, leader of the Russian church. Both Makary and Afanasy had had the good fortune to avoid Ivan's wrath. Perhaps after witnessing the start of the terror in 1565, Afanasy worried that he might not always be so lucky. In any case, he resigned in the spring of 1566, citing ill health.

To fill his vacant position, Ivan chose Philipp Kolychev. An honest and dedicated clergyman, Kolychev had long served as abbot of a monastery on an island in the White Sea, far to the north. Perhaps because of his honesty, not to mention raw courage, he and the tsar immediately got off on the wrong foot. Kolychev said he would become metropolitan on one condition: Ivan must dissolve the *Oprichnina* and call off his black-robed killers. "There must be no *Oprichnina*," the abbot insisted. "I cannot give you my blessing, seeing that the country is in so much anguish."[30]

Not used to such open criticism, the tsar began to fly into one of his well-known rages. But he quickly restrained himself. Evidently he had not reached the point where he felt comfortable killing such a high-ranking clergyman. Needless to say, the meeting ended on a sour note. At first, Kolychev remained firm in refusing the office of metropolitan. But then several boyars and others pleaded with him to take the job. They hoped his good character and strong moral compass would influence Ivan to rule less brutally. Eventually, the abbot gave in and became Metropolitan

Philipp. However, he had to sign an agreement in which he promised to stay out of the tsar's "domestic affairs," which included the *Oprichnina*.

If Philipp had adhered to the agreement, he might have lived to a ripe old age. But his conscience would not allow him to turn a blind eye to the slaughter that was going on around him. He began to criticize the tsar openly. Then, in March 1568 he publicly embarrassed

PHILIPP REFUSES TO BLESS THE TSAR

On a Sunday in March 1568, Ivan and some of his black-robed henchmen attended church and were shocked when the metropolitan Philipp refused to bless the tsar. According to eyewitnesses, Philipp bravely denounced Ivan in front of the congregation, saying in part:

I do not recognize the Orthodox Tsar in this strange dress, and I do not recognize him in the actions of his government. To what limits have you gone, O Tsar, to place yourself beyond the reach of a blessing? Fear the judgment of God, O Tsar! . . . The blood of innocent Christians is being spilled beyond the altar! . . . Even in heathen kingdoms, law and justice prevail, and there compassion for the people—but not here! Here, the lives and possessions of the people are unprotected, everywhere there is pillage, everywhere there is murder, and all this is perpetrated in the name of the Tsar!

Ivan by refusing to offer him blessings in church. Determined now to rid himself of Philipp, the tsar had him arrested and thrown in prison. But the plucky clergyman remained defiant. "Do not torture your people," he roared at Ivan. "Remember always the hour of your death. Depart, O Tsar, from godless acts and remember the fate of former rulers . . . who ruled evily [and] were remembered without pity."[31] By the last months of 1569 Ivan was no longer able to endure Philipp's existence and had him strangled in his cell.

Novgorod Targeted

In his rage, the ruler had stepped over a line that he had long feared to cross. Ivan was deeply immersed in religion and church affairs. And after murdering the leader of Russia's church, he had to be worried about God's anger and swift judgment. Yet days and then weeks went by without any sign of divine displeasure. No thunderbolts hurtled down from the sky to punish the tsar. Nor did the ground open up and swallow him. In his twisted mind, he may have concluded that God had approved of Philipp's removal.

In any case, Ivan must have reasoned that if he could get away with killing the metropolitan, he could get away with almost anything. Indeed, he could go so far

75

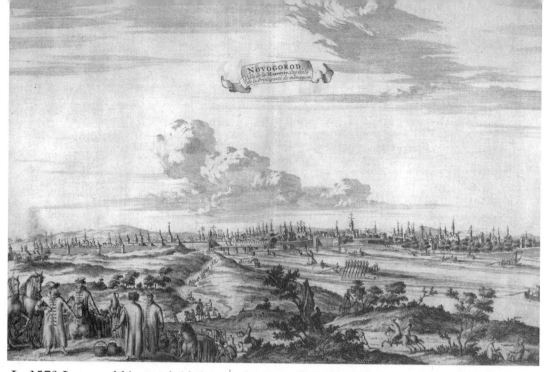

In 1570 Ivan and his men laid siege to the town of Novgorod, whose inhabitants the tsar accused of disloyalty to the crown.

as to destroy an entire city and all of its inhabitants. For a long time he had disliked and distrusted the people of Novgorod. Older than Moscow, in prior centuries Novgorod had been independent and the principal city of northern Russia. Even after Ivan's grandfather conquered them in the 1400s, the Novgorodians remained proud of their past. And they retained a certain air of individuality and separateness from Muscovite culture and affairs.

To Ivan, these traits were signs of treachery against Moscow and the tsar. He came to believe that the people of Novgorod must be punished. Suspicions that were in reality baseless were to him more than enough reason to condemn thousands of people to death. But he knew that many Russians would demand a more concrete reason. So he made up one. The official line became that Novgorod was conspiring to break away from Russia and give its allegiance to Poland's King Sigismund Augustus.

A few of the leading *oprichniki* were reluctant to take part in the attack on Novgorod. They were perfectly willing to kill any individual suspected of posing a danger to their master, but they did not understand the need for eradicating an entire city. These men may have thought that their membership in the secret police gave them the right to question the tsar's decisions. But they were sorely mistaken. All those who expressed doubts about the upcoming expedition ended up in prison or dead.

Mass Death on the Volkhov

Having coldly disposed of the men who had only recently been his trusted confidants, Ivan was ready to strike. In late December 1569 he led an army northward toward Novgorod and its unsuspecting inhabitants. The tsar's forces consisted in part of several thousand *oprichniki*, who surrounded and protected him. Backing up these core followers were more than 10,000 regular army troops.

Ivan wanted to make sure that the Novgorodians did not receive any warning of their impending doom. So it was necessary to keep the army's existence and movements as secret as possible. To this end, Ivan issued some grim orders. All people that the marchers encountered on their journey were to be killed. The *oprichniki* followed these orders to the letter. Farmers and merchants who happened to be transporting their goods on the same road were seized and swiftly murdered. And when the army reached the small town of Klin, the *oprichniki* slaughtered all the inhabitants. A few days later, the residents of the town of Tver, on the Volga River, met a similar fate. More than 9,000 people died, including women, children, and the elderly.

On January 2, 1570, Ivan received word that the army was nearing its primary target, Novgorod, on the Volkhov River. He sent a large detachment of soldiers ahead to surround the city. That way, none of the so-called traitors who dwelled there would be able to escape his righteous wrath. All of the monasteries in the area were shut down and their monks rounded up. Following Ivan's orders, the *oprichniki* beat more than 500 priests day and night with sticks and whips. Only those few who managed to pay their captors large sums of money or gold were allowed to go free. Eventually,

Peasants in Novgorod watch helplessly as Ivan and his men ravage the city.

the tsar had the rest of the monks, and the nuns, too, beaten to death with clubs.

Then it was time for the city's inhabitants to suffer. Some were brought before the tsar. He questioned them and demanded to know about their secret plans to join the Polish king. Since this story had been fabricated by Ivan himself, they had no idea what he was talking about. Still, under torture some confessed to crimes they had not committed. They and many others were condemned to death. The tsar's men built a wooden platform on the main bridge over the Volkhov. Then they began herding the residents, who were bound with ropes, toward it.

IVAN MASSACRES HIS OWN PEOPLE

"Some were to be thrown off the platform, others from the bridge," as Robert Payne tells it.

> The ice had been broken below the bridge, and there was a dark pool of water below. The arms and legs of the victims were bound, and it was thus impossible for them to swim away, and even if they *could* swim, it would not have helped them. Underneath the bridge, the *oprichniki*, armed with boat-hooks, pikes, and axes, were waiting for them in boats. The victims thrown from the bridge sank in the water and then rose to the surface. The *oprichniki* then hacked and chopped them with axes, or thrust at them with pikes and boat-hooks until the bodies sank again.[32]

Some Brave Villagers

The massacre at Novgorod went on without interruption for almost four weeks. Hundreds died each day. The final death toll is unknown and widely disputed by modern scholars. Some have placed it as high as 30,000. Others argue that the entire population of the city was not that high at the time and put the number of dead closer to 15,000. Even if this lower figure is more accurate, Ivan had succeeded in raising the level of his terror campaign to new heights.

Moreover, in his own mind his crusade to rid Russia of traitors to him and God had only begun. In the wake of the slaughter at Novgorod, he began targeting other cities for annihilation. Next on his list was Pskov, west of Novgorod near the border with Livonia. Like Novgorod, Pskov had once been independent and its people clung to their memories of a time when Moscow did not rule them. Pskov was also the most Westernized of Russia's cities, mainly because it lay so close to the kingdoms of eastern Europe. Ivan decided that the city's inhabitants were as guilty as Novgorod's. He also desired to plunder the town's valuables. As had happened at Novgorod, he planned to keep some loot for himself and divide the rest among his dark-robed "brothers."

Ivan enters the gates of Pskov, intent on slaughtering the town's inhabitants.

In this painting, the holy man Mikula, driving a horse-drawn plow, warns Ivan and his men to depart Pskov immediately.

Several smaller towns lay along the route to Pskov, however. Ivan told the *oprichniki* to pillage what they could from these hamlets first. Heinrich von Staden, a German mercenary (hired soldier) who worked with the *oprichniki*, later described what happened in a village whose people refused to go down without a fight:

> We came to a town where there was a church, and my men entered it and took away the icons [holy objects]. . . . Suddenly I saw six horsemen who

were being chased by three hundred [townspeople]. . . . The six horsemen were *oprichniki*. . . . They cried out for help and I attacked [with the rest of my men]. . . . From the upper floor of a house stones were hurled at me [and] I ran up the stairs, an ax in my hands. I was met by a [young woman]. . . . When she observed the anger written on my face, she [tried to run and] I struck her in the back with an ax.[33]

Miracle in Pskov

Despite the bravery of many of the victims, resistance proved futile. The tsar's forces killed nearly everyone they met and soon reached Pskov. There, Ivan immediately had more than 30 local leaders arrested and executed.

However, the larger bloodbath he had been planning did not occur, thanks to what the locals believed was a miracle sent by God. In Pskov Ivan encountered a holy man who was famous throughout western Russia. People called him Mikula. He fearlessly warned the tsar that if he did not leave the town at once, he would regret it. "You feed upon human flesh and blood," Mikula said, "forgetting . . . God himself!"[34]

Ivan would likely have killed the man on the spot had it not been for a strange occurrence. While they were talking, the sky suddenly grew dark and a bolt of lightning struck a nearby tree. Mikula claimed that Pskov was protected by one of God's angels. "A thunderbolt will strike you dead if you or any of your *oprichniki* touch a hair on the head of the smallest child in Pskov,"[35] the holy man said. Only minutes later, one of Ivan's men informed him that his favorite horse had just keeled over and died. Modern observers can rationally call these events coincidences. But the tsar, who was obsessed with divine wrath and other religious notions, was convinced God was sending him a message. Plainly terrified, Ivan actually begged Mikula for forgiveness and ordered his troops to leave Pskov.

Slaughter in Red Square

Whether by coincidence or divine intervention, the people of Pskov had been spared. Many of Ivan's other enemies were not so fortunate, however. In July 1570, having returned to Moscow, he prepared for his next round of butchery. About 300 prisoners had been waiting in Ivan's dungeons for him to punish them. Among the prisoners were several boyars and government administrators and some of the *oprichniki* who had questioned the tsar's decision to attack Novgorod.

Ivan decided to make these men examples by executing them in public. The grim spectacle would take place in Red Square, a large open area in the heart of the city. But on the appointed day, the tsar was disappointed to find he had no audience. The square and nearby streets were deserted. Most Muscovites had heard about the mass murders in Novgorod and were afraid that they might be Ivan's next victims. The truth was that he did not intend to harm them. He only wanted to make sure his bloody show was well attended. Accompanied by several *oprichniki*, he rode up and down the streets demanding that people come out and witness the executions.

Eventually, a large crowd gathered in the square. Frightened and nauseated, the onlookers had to watch a display of carnage that would haunt them ever after. With their razor-sharp swords, the *oprichniki* hacked some of the victims into small pieces. Others were thrown back and forth into big tubs of boiling and freezing water. Soon their skin simply fell off their bones.

The tsar himself participated in the slaughter, confident that the people of Moscow were learning the price they and others would pay for disloyalty. In reality, no

85

one learned anything new. The carnage in Red Square only confirmed what they had already known—their ruler was an inhuman monster. Sooner or later, they reasoned, someone would find a way to kill him. And they prayed it would be sooner rather than later.

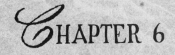
LAST YEARS OF A CRUEL TYRANT

The year 1570 marked an important turning point in the life and reign of Ivan IV. First, his reign of terror reached its height with the mass murders at Novgorod and neighboring towns. Second, and ultimately more important, the tsar was forced to change the major focus of his recent rule. Since establishing the *Oprichnina* in 1565, he had devoted most of his time to internal affairs. Now, quite suddenly, his country came under attack by external forces. After years of going on the offensive against his own people, Ivan found himself on the defensive against enemies that sought to utterly destroy him. Modern historians point out that in large degree he had brought this on himself. While fixated on torturing and killing his own people, he had neglected foreign affairs. The price he and Russia now paid was a heavy one. During the final years of Ivan's reign, both he and his country descended in a downward spiral of misery and despair.

Return of the Tartars

The great turn of events of 1570 shows clearly that what goes on inside a nation can often affect political and military affairs far beyond its borders. Indeed, in making war on his own people Ivan weakened his country. And that inevitably left it vulnerable to outside attack. When the tsar attacked Novgorod it apparently did not occur to him what foreign leaders would make of it. While he fantasized about nonexistent traitors in his midst, very real enemies formed their plans against him.

The most dangerous of these enemies at that time was Devlet Guirey, khan of the Crimean Tartars. Like his predecessors, he saw Russia mainly as a source of loot and slaves. In the early years of Ivan's reign, Guirey remembered, Russia had a strong army and had gone on the offensive. So the Crimean khanate had been unable to make any major headway northward. With the tsar's attention diverted to slaughtering his own people,

A band of Tartars on horseback terrorizes the inhabitants of a Russian village during a small-scale raid.

however, the situation was different. And the khan saw his opportunity to strike.

Guirey was cunning enough to not play his full hand right away. In September 1570 Ivan's messengers informed him that a small force of Tartars—a few thousand at most—had moved into southern Russia. He was worried at first. But these worries soon subsided. News came that, after pillaging a few villages, the intruders had withdrawn. Thus, the incident appeared to be nothing more than a small-scale Tartar raid.

This is what the khan wanted the Russians to think. The raiders were in reality a scouting party sent to test the Russian defenses. Guirey had assembled an army of more than 100,000 men, mostly Tartars with some

89

Turks and other mercenaries mixed in. In April 1571 the enormous horde marched northward and crossed the Russian border. Soon the khan was approached by some Russian nobles who had been in hiding after escaping execution by Ivan. One of them offered to guide the Tartars to Moscow. When he saw that some of Guirey's officers did not trust him, he told them, "If you fail to reach Moscow, then you can impale me! There is nothing standing in your way!"[36]

Ivan first heard of the invasion when word came that the Tartars had burned the city of Tula, not far south of the Oka River. In a state of fear and frenzy, he mustered his trusty henchmen. Several thousand *oprichniki* sped southward while the tsar hurriedly sent word to the scattered units of the main Russian army. He still did not know how large the enemy forces were, and he was alarmed a few days later to learn that a giant Tartar army had crossed the Oka. At this point, Ivan himself was camped only twenty miles away. Terrified, he turned and ran for his life. "Ivan was one of those men who had no difficulty in massacring defenseless civilians," Robert Payne points out. "But he could not command armies or fight, or show courage in adversity. . . . So now, realizing that the Tartars were almost within earshot, he fled."[37]

Moscow in Flames

Ivan had left his *oprichniki* to face the oncoming menace. Though the black riders were formidable against frightened civilians, they were no match for the huge army of veteran Tartar soldiers. Guirey's forces quickly swept the *oprichniki* aside, killing many of them. The survivors fled, as their master had, and the invaders pushed on toward Moscow.

In that city, news of the approaching enemy spread quickly, causing great alarm. Most of the inhabitants at first assumed that the tsar would soon arrive to lead the resistance. But the cowardly Ivan was at that moment still in flight. In fact, he did not stop until he had reached Vologda, a town situated nearly half way to the White Sea. Apparently, he planned that, if needed, he would make his way to that waterway, board a ship, and escape to England. There, he imagined in his tortured mind, Queen Elizabeth I would grant him refuge.

Meanwhile, the boyars who commanded the Russian army rose to the challenge. In the country's hour of need, they, unlike their ruler, showed that they were true patriots. Three large contingents of troops converged near Moscow to defend the city. Unbeknownst to them, however, the Tartars did not intend to lay siege to Moscow. Neither did they desire

The Kremlin burns as Moscow comes under attack. In 1571 the Tartars set fire to the city and then retreated as it burned to the ground.

to get into a major battle with the Russian cavalry. Some brutal fighting did take place south of the city. But before the Russians could fully engage the enemy, the Tartars managed to fulfill their main mission. They set Moscow on fire, then turned away and retreated.

On May 24, 1571, most of the heart of Russia's principal city burned to the ground. As the initial flames spread, a gun factory caught fire and exploded. Burning

IVAN THE TERRIBLE

embers flew far and wide, igniting more buildings. Thousands of people who tried to escape the flames by hiding in cellars suffocated to death. Many others fled into the river and drowned. The next morning, as the smoke cleared, the immensity of the catastrophe began to become clear. Most of the city was now a charred ruin, and more than 60,000 people, fully half of its population, lay dead.

Ivan's Rage

Though extremely dire, this event represented only part of Russia's dilemma. During their retreat, the Tartars looted and burned other towns. They also took many prisoners. At least a hundred thousand Russians were captured and dragged away to become slaves in the Crimea or distant lands.

The blame for these horrors rested largely with the tsar. In his haste to save his own skin, he had not set up a coordinated defense of the country. Yet, as usual, he was quick to shift the blame. Once the Tartars were gone, and he felt he was safe, Ivan returned to Moscow and began to rage against those he claimed had betrayed the country. In particular, he singled out his own *oprichniki*. They had failed him, he said, by allowing the enemy army to make it to Moscow. Leading members of the black riders now found themselves marked for death. Many were executed, while others fled.

To carry out these arrests and executions, Ivan relied partly on lower-ranking *oprichniki*, who remained in his employ a while longer. But more and more he relied on the regular army, which had acquitted itself with distinction during the crisis. Ivan now saw that he badly needed the loyalty of these troops. Not only were they crucial in the crackdown on his former henchmen, but there was still the Tartars to worry about. It was clear that the huge raid they had conducted was only a prelude to more and larger invasions. In fact, the khan now taunted Ivan, sending an envoy with this message:

> I came to Russia, devastated the land and put it to the flames. . . . I desire neither money nor treasure, for they are of no use to me. As for the Tsar, I searched for him everywhere. . . . But you did not come to meet us. . . . You fled from Moscow, and still you dare to call yourself Tsar of Muscovy. You have no shame and are completely without courage. . . . Swear an oath on behalf of yourself, your children, and your grandchildren that you will do as I command. And if you do not do these

things, beware! I have seen the roads . . . of your kingdom and I know the way![38]

Ivan was so upset by these words that he howled at the top of his lungs and tore out sections of his own beard.

Just as the tsar and his advisers expected, Guirey's warning that he "knew the way" into Russia proved a prelude to another invasion. In the summer of 1572 another huge Tartar army pushed northward. This time, however, the Russian generals and their troops were ready to meet the threat. In a tremendous pitched battle, they defeated the khan's forces.

Murder of the Tsarevich

All across Russia, news of the victory set off large-scale celebrations and fervent hymns of thanksgiving. Not surprisingly, Ivan tried to take credit. But he and everyone else knew full well that he had had nothing to do with the victory. His generals had engineered it, especially a boyar named Mikail Vorotynsky. The following year Vorotynsky was arrested, tortured, and executed. The only reason given was that he had supposedly tried to use witchcraft against the tsar, a flimsy and ridiculous charge. Many Russians believed that Ivan slew Vorotynsky out of jealousy and the fear

Ivan cradles his dying son after the tsar, in a fit of rage, attacked the young man with an iron-tipped staff.

that a beloved national hero might be a prime candidate to lead a rebellion against the throne.

Other notable Russians felt the tsar's wrath in the last years of his reign. In the same year that Vorotynsky met his untimely fate, more leading *oprichniki* were killed or fled. Ivan finally decided to disband the dark riders altogether. (He also dissolved the *Oprichnina*.)

None of Ivan's victims in this period was as high ranked and famous as his own son, however. The tsarevich—the next in line for the throne—was also named Ivan. Born in May 1554, he was the second son of Ivan and his first wife, Anastasia. Their third son, Fyodor, had been born three years later, in May 1557. Since Anastasia's death in 1560, Tsar Ivan had married six more times. But these marriages had produced only one other child—a boy born in the 1560s, who had died in infancy. Tsarevich Ivan was therefore Ivan's oldest child. He was also his favorite, which made his death that much more tragic for the tsar.

On November 19, 1581, the younger Ivan, then 27, was present while his father held court at Alexandrova Sloboda. A group of army officers handed the tsar a petition. It asked that he make his eldest son a general and allow him to lead them in the ongoing war in Livonia. For some reason, the tsar mistakenly interpreted this request to mean that the men endorsed the son over the father as a military leader. Flying into a rage, Tsar Ivan called the officers traitors. And soon afterward, he and his son got into a shouting session. In the heat of the moment, the tsar smashed an iron-tipped staff onto his son's head. The young man died three days later.

Descent into Self-Delusion

Overwhelmed with grief and guilt, Ivan never fully emotionally recovered from the tragedy. For months he barely slept. Often he fell off his bed and remained the rest of the night on the floor, moaning. In the daytime he wore only black monk's robes. And at meals or other times he would frequently and suddenly burst into tears and cry for many minutes. Few tried to console him out of fear they would say the wrong thing and suffer the same fate as the tsarevich.

At the same time, Ivan began to display behaviors that were bizarre even for him, a man long given to extraordinary acts. He began to make lists—the *sinodiki*—of his many victims. To compile them, he called in hundreds of scribes. The scribes wrote down not only the names of the dead but also the dates and circumstances of their deaths. In many cases, estates that had been seized from slain boyars were given back to their surviving relatives. It was as if the tsar was desperately trying to atone for his past sins.

Another strange obsession that crept over the ailing ruler involved his fascination with England. He had never been there. Nor had he signed any treaty of alliance with its queen. Yet more and more he became convinced that she would become his benefactor. The long war in Livonia was fast draining Russia's few remaining resources. Ivan fantasized that the English would come to his rescue by supplying him with soldiers and weapons. In addition, Ivan sent an envoy to England to procure him an English wife. None of these products of his descent into self-delusion came even close to becoming reality.

A KINGLY CHALLENGE

In 1581 Ivan exchanged some letters with the king of Poland, who he was at war with. In one, Ivan accused his adversary of allowing Polish soldiers to abuse dead Russians. The king replied in part:

> You accuse me of abusing the dead. I did not abuse them. You, however, torture the living. Which is worse? You condemn me for allegedly breaking the truce! You, the falsifier of treaties, changing them in secret . . .

to satisfy your insane lust for power! We have not set eyes on your face, nor on the flags embroidered with the Cross [of Jesus] which you boast about. You do not frighten your enemies with your Crosses—you frighten only the poor Russians. . . . You say you sorrow over the loss of Christian blood. Well, then, choose a time and place and meet me on horseback and we shall fight one another! God will crown the better one with victory!

Memories of His Misdeeds

Because no help from England ever materialized, Ivan had to deal with the ongoing Livonian conflict himself. The war with Poland and Sweden, then powerful kingdoms, had gone poorly for Russia. In large degree, the failure was due to the tsar's incompetence as a military leader. In desperation, he tried to broker a deal by exchanging letters with the king of Poland. In one, the Polish ruler mocked him and challenged him to single combat. Finally, the tsar realized that victory was impossible and signed treaties, one with Poland in 1582, the other with Sweden the following year. As part of the agreements, Ivan had to give back all the lands he had conquered in the early phases of the war.

On March 17, 1584, a priest makes the sign of the cross over the lifeless body of Ivan the Terrible.

The loss of the war, the death of the tsarevich, and guilt over his many crimes weighed heavily on the tsar. In addition to this emotional burden, he was physically deteriorating at an alarming rate. He was only 53, yet he looked twenty years older. His body was riddled with arthritis, and years of overindulgence in alcohol and rich foods had taken a grim toll. Ivan finally succumbed to his mental and physical ailments on March 17, 1584.

A panel of regents immediately took charge of Russia to ensure a smooth transition while Fyodor prepared to become the new tsar. Even after he was crowned, these men remained close advisers and actually ran the government. This was because Fyodor was physically weak and of limited intelligence. Much unlike his father, he was also a kind and timid person who neither hurt nor murdered anyone. When Fyodor died only fourteen years later, his chief regent-adviser, Boris Godunov, became tsar. Many other tsars followed, until the last was assassinated in 1918.

Fortunately for Russia, none of these rulers earned a reputation for cruelty and brutality that came close to that of the first tsar, Ivan IV. The memories of his misdeeds and near ruin of his country live on. They are a reminder of how one of the world's greatest countries was partly forged in the spilled blood and sacrifice of countless innocent lives.

CHRONOLOGY

1530	Ivan IV Vasilevich is born.
1533	Grand Prince Vasily, Ivan's father, dies. Ivan becomes grand prince, but his mother, Elena, rules as his regent.
1538	Elena, dies. Vasily Shuisky becomes regent. He is later replaced by Ivan Belsky.
1541	Khan Saip Guirey launches unsuccessful invasion of Muscovy. Vasily Shuisky seizes the opportunity to build an army and regain power.
1542	Vasily Shuisky dies. His cousin Andrey Shuisky seizes the position of regent.
1543	Ivan arranges Andrey Shuisky's murder.
1547	Ivan is crowned Tsar of Russia in an elaborate ceremony; less than a month later, he marries Anastasia Zakharina; a fire destroys much of Moscow.
1550	Ivan introduces reforms to the *Sudebnik*, the nation's law code.
1551	Ivan orders an invasion of the Khanate of Kazan.
1552	Ivan begins a series of wars with neighboring nations in an attempt to gain territory; the Khanate of Kazan is conquered; Ivan's first child, Dmitry, is born.
1553	Dmitry dies.
1554	The Russians conquer the Khanate of Astrakhan; Ivan's second son, also named Ivan, is born.
1555	Ivan signs a trade agreement with England.
1557	Ivan's son Fyodor is born.

102

1558	The Russians capture many towns in neighboring Livonia.
1560	Anastasia dies.
1561	To escape the Russian invaders, Livonian cities submit to Polish rule. This results in a protracted war between Russia and Poland.
1564	Ivan has several high-ranking officials murdered. His "reign of terror" begins.
1565	Ivan establishes the *Oprichnina,* a separate kingdom within Russia's borders, to be ruled only by nobles of his choosing, and the *oprichniki,* a special police force loyal only to him.
1566	Ivan orders the arrests of three hundred boyars who protest the actions of the *oprichniki.* More than two thirds of them are tortured and murdered.
1568	Ivan has Metropolitan Philipp imprisoned in retaliation for criticizing him.
1569	Ivan has Philipp strangled; on Ivan's orders, the *oprichniki* march toward the city of Novrogod, killing more than nine thousand people along the way.
1570	Ivan's forces attack Novrogod, killing most of the city's inhabitants; Ivan has three hundred men publicly tortured and executed in Red Square
1571	The Crimean Khanate invades Russia and burns most of Moscow to the ground, killing more than half of the city's inhabitants.
1581	Ivan murders his son Ivan in a fit of rage.
1582	Ivan signs a peace treaty with Poland, ending the decades-old Livonian war.
1584	Ivan dies. His son Fyodor becomes the new tsar.

GLOSSARY

Boyar Duma: A council of leading boyars that advised the tsar.

boyars: Members of the nobility in early Russia.

icons: Religious articles considered sacred in Orthodox Christianity.

mercenary: A hired soldier.

metropolitan: The highest office in the Russian Orthodox Church.

Muscovy: The kingdom established by the grand princes of Moscow in the 15th and 16th centuries. The term became synonymous with early Russia.

oprichniki: Ivan's army of henchmen, who wore black robes and committed various atrocities at his orders.

Oprichnina: A sort of kingdom within a kingdom, essentially a separate political unit Ivan set up inside Russia.

serdechniki: Ghouls, zombies, or evil spirits widely thought to cause disaster and mischief.

sinodiki: Lists of the dead.

Sudebnik: Russia's law code, which Ivan reformed.

tsar (or czar): The supreme ruler of Russia (from the Latin term *Caesar*, a title used by the Roman emperors).

tsarevich: The tsar's eldest son and heir to Russia's throne.

zemshchina: The term Ivan adopted to describe the lands and people existing outside his *Oprichnina*.

SOURCE NOTES

Introduction: The Bloodbath Begins

1. Albert Schlichting, *A Brief Account of the Rule of the Tyrant Ivan Grozny*, trans. A.I. Malein. Leningrad, Russia, 1934, p. 25.

2. Quoted in Schlichting, *Brief Account*, pp. 38–39.

Chapter 1: Ivan's Childhood and Rise to Power

3. Quoted in Andrei Pavlov and Maureen Perrie, *Ivan the Terrible*. London: Pearson, 2003, p. 27.

4. Nicholas V. Riasanovsky, *A History of Russia*. New York: Oxford University Press, 1984, p. 143.

5. Quoted in J.L. Fennel Jr., ed., *The Correspondence Between Prince A.M. Kurbsky and Tsar Ivan IV of Russia, 1564–1579*. Cambridge, England: Cambridge University Press, 1955, pp. 72–73.

6. Quoted in Fennel, *Correspondence*, pp. 74–75.

7. Quoted in *Nikon Chronicle*, Moscow: Iazyki Russkoi Kultury, 1904, vol. 13, p. 434.

8. Robert Payne and Nikita Romanoff, *Ivan the Terrible*. New York: Thomas

Y. Crowell, 1975, p. 58.

Chapter 2: Tsar, Husband, and Reformer

9. Quoted in Payne and Romanoff, *Ivan the Terrible*, p. 67.

10. Payne and Romanoff, *Ivan the Terrible*, p. 75.

11. Quoted in Payne and Romanoff, *Ivan The Terrible*, pp. 88–89.

12. Pavlov and Perrie, *Ivan the Terrible*, pp. 61–62.

13. Quoted in Warren B. Walsh, ed., *Readings in Russian History*. 3 vols. Syracuse, NY: Syracuse University Press, 1963, vol. 1, p. 109.

Chapter 3: Ivan Attempts to Build an Empire

14. Quoted in *Nikon Chronicle*, vol. 13, pp. 184–85, 483.

15. Quoted in *Nikon Chronicle*, vol. 13, pp. 203, 499.

16. Payne and Romanoff, *Ivan the Terrible*, pp. 125–26.

17. Quoted in *Kazansky Chronicle*. Moscow, 1954, pp. 443–44.

18. Quoted in Walsh, *Readings in*

Russian History, vol. 1 p. 77

19. Quoted in Soloviev, *Istoriya Rossii*, vol. 3, p. 519.

20. Quoted in *Nikon Chronicle*, vol. 13, pp. 524–25.

Chapter 4: The Tsar Adopts Rule by Terror

21. Pavlov and Perrie, *Ivan the Terrible*, p. 159.

22. Payne and Romanoff, *Ivan the Terrible*, p. 220.

23. Quoted in *Nikon Chronicle*, vol. 13, p. 393.

24. Quoted in M.G. Roginsky, trans., "Poslaniye Taube i Kruse," *Russian Historical Journal*, vol. 8, 1922, p. 22.

25. Quoted in Roginsky, "Poslaniye Taube i Kruse," p. 35.

26. Quoted in Roginsky, "Poslaniye Taube i Kruse," p. 35.

27. Payne and Romanoff, *Ivan the Terrible*, p. 249.

28. J.L. Fennell Jr., ed., *Prince Kurbsky's History of Ivan IV*. Cambridge, England: Cambridge University Press, 1965, p. 208.

Chapter 5: Ivan Massacres His Own People

29. Quoted in Roginsky, "Poslaniye Taube i Kruse," p. 41.

30. Quoted in N.M. Karamazin, *Istoriya Gosudarsive Rossiiskogo*. 10 vols. St. Petersburg, Russia: A. Smirdin, 1833–1835, vol. 9, pp. 91–92.

31. Quoted in Payne and Romanoff, *Ivan the Terrible*, p. 259.

32. Payne and Romanoff, *Ivan the Terrible*, p. 278.

33. Heinrich von Staden, *The Land and Government of Muscovy*, trans. T. Esper. Palo Alto, CA: Stanford University Press, 1967, pp. 120–21.

34. Quoted in Staden, *The Land and Government of Muscovy*, pp. 27–28.

35. Quoted in Edward Bond, *Russia at the Close of the Sixteenth Century*. London: Hakluyt Society, 1856, p. 161.

Chapter 6: Last Years of a Cruel Tyrant

36. Quoted in A.A. Zimin, *The Oprichnina of Ivan the Terrible*. Moscow, 1964, p. 452.

37. Payne and Romanoff, *Ivan the Terrible*, p. 309.

38. Quoted in Karamazin, *Istoriya Gosudarsive Rossiiskogo*, vol. 9, pp. 181–82.

FOR MORE INFORMATION

Books

Alan Axlerod and Charles Phillips, *Dictators and Tyrants: Absolute Rulers and Would-Be Rulers in World History*. New York: Facts On File, 1995.

Thomas G. Butson, *Ivan the Terrible*. New York: Chelsea House, 1987.

James P. Duffy and Vincent L. Ricci, *Czars: Russia's Rulers for More than One Thousand Years*. New York: Facts On File, 1995.

Michael Kort, *Russia*. New York: Facts On File, 2004.

James E. Strickler, Russia of the Tsars. San Diego: Lucent, 1998.

Web Sites

History of Russia (www.geographia.com/russia/rushis01.html). A worthwhile site that contains numerous links leading to short but informative articles about various periods of Russian history.

Ivan IV of Russia (www.xs4all.nl/~kvenjb/madrus.htm #grosny). A brief, easy-to-read overview of Ivan's life and major deeds, with a useful bibliography for those who want to find more detailed accounts.

Ivan IV Vasilyevich (http://encarta.msn.com/encyclo pedia_761561311/Ivan_IV_vasilyevich.html). This excellent brief overview of the main points of Ivan's life and reign was written by a noted authority on Ivan, Richard Hellie of the University of Chicago.

INDEX

PICTURE CREDITS

ABOUT THE AUTHOR

Historian Don Nardo has published many volumes for young readers about ancient and medieval civilizations, including *The Roman Empire, Life in Ancient Athens, The Etruscans, The Byzantine Empire, The Vikings, The Mongol Empire*, and *Weapons and Warfare of the Middle Ages*. He lives in Massachusetts with his wife, Christine.